D0282776

The Unconventional Manager

THE KEY TO REAL SUCCESS ...
SWIM AGAINST THE TIDE!

Ron Haberkorn

FOUNDER OF NOREX, INC.

PAD Publishing
Prior Lake, Minnesota
www.TheUnconventionalManager.com

PAD Publishing
5505 Cottonwood Lane SE
Prior Lake, MN 55372
Internet: www.TheUnconventionalManager.com
E-mail: info@TheUnconventionalManager.com

The Unconventional Manager is available at Amazon.com or may be ordered from your local bookseller. Quantity discounts also are available. Contact PAD Publishing at the above address or visit www.TheUnconventionalManager.com

DEDICATION

*This book is dedicated to my business partner,
cheerleader, consultant, guidance counselor, best friend,
and wife, Sandy! Without Sandy there would be no book,
no successful company, nor a wonderful, loving family.
Thank you, Sandy, for putting up with me all of these years!*

TABLE OF CONTENTS

GUARANTEE OF
UNCONVENTIONAL ACCESS

Other authors typically would not publish their direct contact information in their book, and that is precisely the reason I am doing so. Below I have listed my personal e-mail address and direct phone number in addition to my direct mailing address. My reason for giving this unusual access is because it is fun to "swim against the tide" of what others are doing. It is important to live up to what this book is all about. Plus, I am confident that everyone will get at least one good idea from this book, and that all readers will be satisfied. My goal is 100% reader satisfaction!

Thanks for buying the book!

Ron

Ron Haberkorn
5505 Cottonwood Lane SE
Prior Lake, MN 55372
E-mail: ron@norex.net
Phone: 952-447-8898 ext. 235
Internet: www.TheUnconventionalManager.com

ACKNOWLEDGEMENTS

I am incredibly appreciative to so many individuals for their support throughout my life and certainly in the creation of this book. I am deeply grateful to:

My wife, Sandy, for her suggestions, editing, and general support in shaping and molding this book.

Chuck Wetherall for his help in writing drafts of the book and for coordinating the publishing. Without your encouragement, Chuck, there would be no book.

Deb Kind, our daughter, for her internal and external book design. To both Deb and Steve Kind for suggestions while proofing and editing the book.

Dave Van Lear for offering the idea for the NOREX business plan. All of us on the NOREX Team have benefited from your idea and generosity.

Ken Rapp at IC System for being the first NOREX customer. And to John Erickson for giving Ken the go-ahead!

John Miller for being our first and extremely successful team member. One hire and one fabulous individual! What are the odds?

Bob Barsness president of Prior Lake State Bank for giving us a 3rd mortgage on our house during those early years.

Dan Alderson for offering the idea that was the genesis of the Never Again principle.

All NOREX customers too numerous to mention, past and present, who have encouraged us to stay on the path of unconventional management in everything we do.

All NOREX team members (employees) past and present who have helped mold *The Unconventional Manager* philosophy, and in addition have offered encouragement, content, and support for this book.

And most importantly, I thank God for guiding me in my life and on the venture called NOREX.

UNCONVENTIONAL FOREWORD

The foreword is normally written by a high profile VIP to give the author credibility. I can't think of a better way to give credibility to the principles in this book than by using an unsolicited note received from one of our customers:

"I'm writing for three purposes. First, I want to tell you what an excellent experience I had at the forum yesterday in St. Louis. I had very high expectations going into it, based on reports from previous attendees. Those expectations were met and exceeded. The facilitation was excellent and the day moved fast, covering a lot of material. Even the snacks and lunch were great.

It was helpful to benchmark our own performance in relation to what other organizations are doing when facing similar challenges. It is especially helpful to learn where people have found good solutions and where others have had difficulties with vendors or technologies. The service you provide, in facilitating the sharing of experience with no sales pitches, is just a great business model.

Second, I want to thank you and NOREX for extending our membership for several months this year while we have been in transition. We will be sending the renewal payment as soon as we can process it.

Third, I want to tell you how impressed I am by the NOREX Pledge. The sections for Members / Customers and Vendors sound somewhat like the words from some other organizations, but I was especially impressed with the following two sections.

To Team Members: A stable family-friendly environment is a critical element of our present and future success. Employment fairness and stability outrank profit as our primary goal. Adequate profit (not maximum) will result.

Financial performance will vary from quarter to quarter and year to year. It is the obligation of management/ownership to 'flex' as required to achieve maximum employment security.

To Country and Community: We are deeply thankful to our country and community for fostering an environment where NOREX can thrive.We show our appreciation through positive involvement in the community and annual charitable giving of over 5% of profits before tax.

The goal of adequate profit, not maximum, and a commitment to the community, not based on maximizing profit, are admirable and rare. I see that NOREX is not a public corporation and that explains how it is possible to put this philosophy into action.

I also looked at your ad for an Account Executive position and saw this: 'In addition, we are seeking an individual with a strong personal commitment to high moral and ethical standards.'

I have seen this commitment, and the embodiment of the pledge, in action in our dealings with NOREX. Please accept my thanks and admiration of your organization."

Gary Lyndaker
IT Director for the Missouri Department of Mental Health

It is letters like this that have inspired me to share the NOREX story and our approach to being *The Unconventional Manager.*

Ron

Ron Haberkorn

WITH THE TIDE

"The end justifies the means."
"Rules are made to be broken."
"A little fib never hurt anybody."
"Some feelings will be hurt."

AGAINST THE TIDE

*"Get out in front" by establishing
a strong organizational culture
of fairness, respect, integrity and
compassion that applies to everyone!
Even the top executive!*

NOTE: AT THE BEGINNING OF EACH CHAPTER ARE "WITH THE TIDE" AND
"AGAINST THE TIDE" STATEMENTS THAT CONTRAST THE THINKING OF
CONVENTIONAL AND UNCONVENTIONAL MANAGERS.

CHAPTER 1

The Beginning

Numerous scandals have rocked our government, business, political, and religious organizations in recent years. Clearly something basic is very, very wrong!

We read daily about sex scandals involving governors, mayors, CEOs, religious leaders, schoolteachers, managers, and even U.S. presidents. How can these people be such hypocrites?

Is it right for politicians to distort what their opponents say? And when confronted have a flimsy "well it's politics" excuse? What happened to the values of honesty and fair play?

Many feel cheating "a little bit" is harmless and that the end justifies the means. Is it okay to break the law? Does it depend on which law? Is it okay to break the law a little bit? How do you decide? Is the law situational? And how do we teach our kids riding in the car with us to respect laws when we don't? Do they get a message that it is okay to ignore laws when they don't agree with them? Do you want your kids to try illegal drugs because they think cheating just once or twice is okay?

As we all know, people who get away with dishonesty once often think they can do it again and again and not get caught. And when they inevitably get caught in a "big one" they respond with, "I just did it once." And a scandal ensues.

People we hold in high regard today may someday be similarly exposed and disappoint everyone they know. Before they are caught, many of these people espouse a holier-than-thou attitude. And tomorrow who knows what else: tax cheating, immoral behavior, or pushing the legal system to the very edge? Is this what we want? Is this what we want for our organizations?

> *We all need to be sure we are keeping our house in order.*

If not, we all need to be sure we are keeping our house in order. People and organizations are losing their moral compasses on doing what is right ... JUST BECAUSE IT IS RIGHT.

> *People and organizations are losing their moral compasses on doing what is right ... JUST BECAUSE IT IS RIGHT.*

QUICK TO CRITICIZE

When we read about these transgressions, we are quick to criticize the behavior. But what preventive measures are we taking in our own organizations to discourage or eliminate the potential for such scandals? Action must be taken before the scandals hit! Each of us needs to do our part to improve our organization. Within our sphere of control we can clearly define a culture that minimizes the potential for such behavior. But what specific things can we do to eliminate these behaviors in our organizations? I challenge you to take ideas from this book, get out in front, and prevent problems before they occur!

Management can expect employees to be only as honest and ethical as they are!

UNBELIEVABLE

While attending a meeting at a local university, I spoke informally with a professor about the importance of honest and ethical conduct in business. I couldn't believe his response. He said, "It is easy to be honest and ethical when you are successful ... but quite another story when one is just starting out." I absolutely couldn't believe it! And this comment came from someone who is teaching our young adults!

A BETTER WAY

During the first months of NOREX's existence, we made a commitment to our new customers that they would not be billed until NOREX reached 25 members. In our third month, I visited with the Mayo Clinic in Rochester, MN, and they decided to join as member number eight. As Mayo went through the sign-off process, somehow a check was issued and mailed to NOREX. It was quite a surprise as this was absolutely the first revenue we had ever received!

I called my contact at Mayo and explained to him that we should not have received the payment until the membership reached twenty-five. I offered to send him a refund check for the amount paid. He refused saying, "it would be more work getting the money back into Mayo than it is worth." He remained a loyal member for years before his retirement.

So ... it doesn't matter if you can afford it or not. It is absolutely critical that one maintains impeccable ethics and honesty! And with similar early decisions at NOREX, the foundation was laid for the organization.

In reality, whether one is starting out or already successful, it is equally critical to be honest and ethical! First, because an honest person cannot "turn it on and off." Second, because the foundation is laid with employees for future behavior. Third, because success is absolutely dependent on it. And last, simply BECAUSE IT IS MORALLY RIGHT!

HOW WE SURVIVED

The survival rate of new businesses is incredibly low, and many businesses that do survive sometimes achieve their goal at the expense of key interpersonal values ... respect, fairness, integrity, and compassion. On the other hand, NOREX has remained true to its unconventional values while swimming against the tide (of what everyone else is doing) and has become successful beyond my expectations!

Built on important key principles, NOREX has become an organization respected by our team members, our customers, our vendors, and our community. We call these principles unconventional because all too often it seems organizations put their primary emphasis on the bottom line, while at the same time giving only "lip service" to caring about employees, customers, and vendors. Obviously there are exceptions. Still we know that management is commonly perceived by employees and the public as having one focus: Profit/Productivity!

ANCHOR POINT #1

The unconventional manager principles outlined in this book will reduce the probability of scandals in your organization.

NOTE: EACH CHAPTER OF THE BOOK IS SUMMARIZED WITH AN "ANCHOR POINT."
A KEY INSIGHT THAT WILL KEEP YOU GROUNDED ON WHAT IS IMPORTANT.

WITH THE TIDE

Profit/productivity is the all-encompassing reason for an organization to exist. All other priorities pale in comparison.

AGAINST THE TIDE

With a primary focus on the people, profit/productivity will result.

CHAPTER 2

People #1...
Profit/Productivity #2

WHY WRITE A BOOK?

I am writing this book because I believe students, entrepreneurs, managers, and leaders in all areas of our society need encouragement to resist the temptations of radical self-interest and "success at any price." It is written for honest people with the intent of giving them the courage to swim against the tide of the "everyone-else-is-doing-it" mantra in our society.

I am not an author. I am not an intellectual. My only qualification to write this book is that in 1980 I started a company using unconventional principles, and it has succeeded beyond my wildest dreams.

The NOREX team encouraged me to write this book.

The intent is to illustrate the management principles that guided the success of our modest "laboratory" in Minnesota called NOREX. I have learned that you don't need to be glib or sophisticated to be successful. And you don't need a degree from Wharton or Harvard. However, going "against the tide" is a satisfying path to success.

This book is neither a magic pill, nor a silver bullet. Rather it is about sharing the ideas and basic concepts used to develop a squeaky-clean culture with an *unconventional management approach.*

PERSONAL BACKGROUND

I was born and raised in a middle class neighborhood in south Minneapolis. I excelled in a few areas but was totally average in most others. However, I knew the difference between right and wrong.

I was an active participant in high school, serving on committees that were a part of our student government. My college years were spent in my hometown where I graduated from the University of Minnesota with a B.S. in Business Administration.

> *I knew the difference between right and wrong.*

My education continued through 20 years of hands-on business experience with several large, high-quality, local companies. Among them Northwestern Bell Telephone Co. (now Qwest), and 17 years with Control Data Corp. Before

I went into sales for
Control Data, I thought
all sales people were
liars, cheats, drunks, and
joke tellers! Of course
they weren't, but that
was my perception. I
decided to go into sales

*For Christmas,
give boxes of candy for
the entire organization to
share rather than a bottle
of scotch for an individual!*

for Control Data and be unconventional. And it worked! For
example: For Christmas I gave boxes of candy for the entire
organization to share rather than a bottle of scotch for an
individual!

THE BEGINNING

In 1980 I started a company called North American
Computer Exchange (later renamed NOREX, Inc). On the
first day I was the only full-time employee with my wife,
Sandy, serving part time as office "hunt and peck" secretary.
We financed our fragile start-up with a second mortgage,
and later, a third mortgage on our house.

This idea of an information technology (IT) consortium
actually was suggested to me by one of my Control Data customers. We regularly sold computer equipment to Norwest
Bank (now merged with Wells Fargo). Over the years of selling
for Control Data, my approach was to focus on caring for my
customers and prospective customers. My annual sales quota
was easily exceeded as a result of that approach.

During one of my visits to Norwest, Dave Van Lear (a

> *Dave never would have offered this idea had I not earned his respect as a fair and honest player.*

highly-respected data processing executive) suggested that I should consider forming a business linking IT professionals together to buy and sell used computer equipment and solve the common problems that confronted them. I am absolutely positive that Dave never would have offered this idea had I not earned his respect as a fair and honest player.

THE IDEA TAKES ROOT

The moment he suggested this business model, I sensed I was on the threshold of something with great potential. Still there were many hurdles to overcome. I had to convince my wife, Sandy, as well as myself, that the time was right to pursue this idea. We had four daughters: two in grade school and two in college! Looking back, I still am amazed that I actually had the guts to quit my job at Control Data and take on the challenge of a start-up operation.

We rented a small office and furnished it with two government surplus type wooden desks. We hauled them home in the family station wagon and brought them to life in our garage with a coat of varnish. A few more used odds and ends were purchased to make the place functional.

"Baby steps" was the name of the game, a principle I will discuss in later chapters. Frankly, we didn't have the money for rapid growth, and I am thankful we didn't! Likely I would have "burned through it" and had little to show for it.

I confess that my family got short-changed during this time. I was scared stiff and worked days, nights, and weekends to succeed! I had a tiger by the tail and just could not let go!

First year sales were modest, but growth was slow and steady. Year after year NOREX grew moderately and added employees (we call them "team members"). Thus was born the "baby step, self-financed approach" to growth.

It was in these early years that I learned we needed nice people, and we needed them to be productive in order to survive! Without the

> *The baby step, self-financed approach to growth works!*

people there would be no organization or profit! So we treat our team well, not only to minimize turnover, but because "it is just the right thing to do"!

NOREX TODAY

Currently NOREX is a unique consortium of IT professionals from over 1,500 organizations across the U.S. and Canada. Throughout the years we have counted 195 Fortune 500 companies as customers. We currently serve 348 local, state, and federal government entities. There are no other organizations quite like NOREX. Still, by most measurements, we are a small company with fewer than 60 team members and

> *We provide IT professionals <u>a better way</u> of leveraging each others' experiences.*

annual revenue of about $7 million.

Simply put, our customers share real-world experiences, strategies, and solutions in order to avoid reinventing the wheel and avoid costly missteps. We provide IT professionals (those who handle the backroom technology of computer-based information systems) a better way of leveraging each others' experiences ... regardless of industry, size of installation, or the technical environment.

MY HOPE FOR THIS BOOK

This book is written for ethical managers who are receptive to new ideas as they strive to provide a work environment where the foundation is respect, integrity, fairness, and compassion. We share insights that have worked well for our company over the last 25-plus years. By applying the principles in this book, our start-up company has prospered and exceeded well beyond our initial goals! I believe the principles will help your organization as well!

My hope is that my philosophies (yes, Judeo-Christian principles) will resonate with managers at all levels in business, government, and non-profits. This book will also be helpful to college students needing reinforcement to stay focused on honesty and integrity in their future careers.

I do not pretend that the principles in this book will be

easy and effective in all workplace settings. For example, a manager in a large organization may have some limitations based on strict policies. However, with some creativity and determination, many of the principles will fit within a department and not be in conflict with policies. Many of the concepts involve little or no cost. Plus, our "against the tide" principles may provide the encouragement needed to work toward revision of restrictive policies.

Apply the concepts of *The Unconventional Manager* to your organization or your department, and you will create an opportunity to achieve your aspirations ... and you'll do it in the most honest and satisfying way possible. You can become a better manager and a better person as well. What has worked for us can work for you in your organization.

ANCHOR POINT #2

Focus first on people and then profit/productivity. Long-term sustainability will result.

WITH THE TIDE

Do the right thing until there is a situation when it is "necessary" to bend the rules in order to achieve organizational goals.

AGAINST THE TIDE

Do the right thing in all situations ...no matter what!

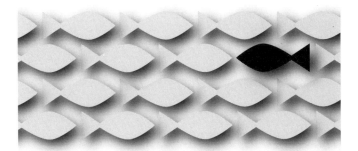

CHAPTER 3

Do The Right Thing

The Unconventional Manager **is not a model based on the laws of reciprocation** in which one person provides a benefit to another simply because he or she expects something in return. Rather, it is a model based on, "What would mother have me do?" My mother, and probably yours, definitely believed in "DOING THE RIGHT THING NO MATTER WHAT."

The satisfying, safe, sure, and fun path to success is to create a culture that is unconventional ... free from questionable ethics and committed to uncompromising respect, fairness, integrity, and compassion for all.

> *Create a culture that is unconventional ... free from questionable ethics and committed to uncompromising respect, fairness, integrity, and compassion for all.*

NO NEED TO APOLOGIZE

Managers who follow the squeaky-clean path are sometimes made to feel like outsiders, even ashamed, to choose the narrower, straighter path to business success. Sometimes they are apologetic in the defense of their moral choices. They face tremendous pressure to conform to someone else's view of morality and honesty, and are often coerced to go along with the crowd down the slippery road of deceit.

What is critically important is that the spirit of respect, fairness, integrity, and compassion comes from your heart. If you're doing the right thing, but inwardly believe otherwise, you're only fooling yourself. Your true intentions will quickly become apparent to your co-workers.

It takes inner strength and belief to withstand contemporary pressures and stand up for one's integrity. It takes even greater strength to do so proudly and unapologetically.

COURAGE TO ACT

The principles of this book are straightforward and easy to understand. But the devil is in the details: One needs the belief and courage to be different! Why? Because in many organizations the philosophy of *The Unconventional Manager* runs counter to prevailing attitudes.

The world may think "squeaky clean" is nerdy or square, but, unconventional managers choose to think it is not only right, but is the least stressful, and most rewarding path to sustained success. It works ... and it works well.

DOING WHAT IS RIGHT

Complete honesty and openness are easier than the alternative. You can feel good about yourself for having the courage and satisfaction

> *The "squeaky clean" principle is not nerdy or square ... it is the least stressful, and most rewarding path to success.*

of doing what is right. And honesty does not require a good memory ... there is no need to track when you might have "stretched the truth," because you always think and act in a consistent, straightforward way.

When the unconventional manager is concerned with doing what is right, he or she is not only a kinder leader, but a more effective one as well. Plus, such a manager can sleep at night with a clear conscience!

If you tell the truth, you have less to remember!

> *If you tell the truth, you have less to remember!*

TO THE FUTURE

The unconventional principles can easily be applied whether your leadership is from the plush, corner office on the executive level or in the basement mailroom. But to enjoy the riches it produces, you simply must have the faith to try it. Only then will you understand and experience its value.

ANCHOR POINT #3

Relax and sleep at night with a clear conscience knowing that you are absolutely committed to doing what is right in all situations.

WITH THE TIDE

Workplace cultures "just happen"
and are beyond the control of
management.

AGAINST THE TIDE

*Clearly define the key elements
of an ethical culture from the
top down so the loudest and most
manipulative employees don't!*

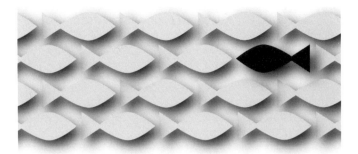

CHAPTER 4

Building The Culture

What makes an organization successful in the long run comes from within the leaders of the organization who are guided by higher and superior ethical values. Yes, values based on the discipline of moral duty and obligation, and most notably what is right and wrong. NOREX key values are:

- **Integrity:** Fairness and justice which refuses to lie or deceive in any way.

- **Fairness:** Impartiality and honesty, free from self-interest, prejudice, or favoritism.

- **Compassion:** Sympathetic concern for others' distress, together with a desire to help.

- **Ethics:** Dealing with what is good and bad using a set of moral principles.

- **Respect:** Weighing the views and desires of others and consideration of that information into decisions and behaviors.

If management exemplifies and allows profanity, office romances, excessive use of alcohol, or other anti-social behaviors, that message flows throughout the organization and affects everyone. In contrast, having a zero tolerance for anything that is "not right" creates an ethical culture.

From the very beginning, NOREX set out to purposefully create a positive culture, rather than leave this crucial pillar of organizational strength to chance. When we started, we had but two employees and had no need for written cultural rules. As we grew, we discovered we needed to document our cultural elements, and we developed written policies. For example, the following are some NOREX cultural elements and our abbreviated policies on each:

Key Values:
Integrity
Fairness
Compassion
Ethics
Respect

- **Smoke-Free Environment:** No smoking in the building.
- **Treatment of Others:** We treat each other with respect, honesty, fairness, and compassion.
- **Office Romances:** Don't even think about it! Flirting with a married team member is not in the best interest of the individuals, their families, or the organization.

- **Profanity:** None. No one should have to endure profanity in the workplace.
- **Sexual Harassment:** Again, don't even think about it! No one should ever be subjected to sexual harassment of any kind.
- **Alcohol Usage:** None in the building. We give two drink tickets for some off-site functions.
- **Dress Code:** Whether business or casual, always professional.

TEAM MEMBERS "BUY INTO" THE CULTURE

We communicate these elements by showing a NOREX culture video to prospective team members. Plus, we also periodically show the video to the entire team. New team member growth and understanding occur as team members socialize with each other and offer tips, tactics, and stories about the culture. They learn about what is expected and what is not. New team members quickly learn how to fit into the culture of the organization. Over time they develop trust and belief that NOREX is truly different than any other place they have worked.

> *Team members accept and even enhance the culture, and some seek out others to join them in the organization.*

A few have not felt comfortable with our culture and eventually left to seek employment elsewhere. We accepted their decisions gracefully as the right thing for them and NOREX. In no case will we compromise our values to retain team members.

Our team members accept and even enhance the culture. In fact, some seek out others to join them in the organization.

MULTIPLE ADVANTAGES

There are many, many advantages to a positive culture. A new level of trust develops. Team members view themselves more as capitalists than captives. They "own" their jobs and respect them. Not surprisingly, they take better care of what they own than what they rent.

They exert maximum efforts in times of need. If computers crash or work becomes backlogged, both unconventional managers and their unconventional team instinctively put their shoulders to the wheel without being prodded to do so.

> *Customers believe you care about their best interests, because you and the entire organization really do care.*

They know that management is *compassionate and trustworthy* and not only looks out for their welfare, but the welfare of their families as well.

Customers believe you care about their best interests, because you and the entire organization really do care!

Vendors are amazed that you are willing to let them make a profit. And senior management appreciates the "no complaints" and "no lawsuit" aspect of the culture, as well as the public relations benefits of having a first-rate organization.

COST SAVINGS

No manager needs to be told how employee turnover can destroy productivity. According to the U.S. Department of Labor 2007 statistics, the professional and business service industry had an annual turnover rate of about 50%, with an average rate of 53% per year over a five-year period (2003-2007). In contrast, NOREX turnover was 2% in 2007 with a five-year average of 11% per year. In other words, over the five-year period NOREX experienced 79% less turnover than others in our industry!

We estimate the loss of each employee can be valued at approximately 150% of their annual wage or salary (because of reduced productivity, new employee training, and a host of other issues). In other words, you can realize the enormous opportunity for time and dollar savings. Time is better spent improving processes rather than training new people.

A SELF-POLICING ENVIRONMENT

As effective as the system of unconventional management may seem, it is never perfect. Some will challenge or push the concepts of respect, honesty, fairness, and compassion. But the culture automatically responds to employees who miss the message. Rarely will management have to counsel an associate for not putting in an honest day's work. When profanity in the workplace is discouraged by the culture, employees will get the message from other employees. If an employee comes to work wearing clothing unsuitable to the workplace, the examples shown by fellow employees make the offender aware of dress guidelines.

Sadly, some team members who have left NOREX come to understand the value of the culture only after they join other organizations.

> *Some team members who have left NOREX come to understand the value of the culture only after they join other organizations.*

The benefits of a "squeaky-clean" positive culture accrue to everyone. It is not the exclusive domain of senior management; everyone in all relationships can use it. The manager of a three-person department can manage an unconventional department, free from morale problems and brimming with teamwork and camaraderie. Likewise, the benefits will accrue to the VP of an international division, or the entrepreneur just starting a business.

NET, NET

The benefits of a positive culture are almost too abundant to enumerate, but in the following chapters I will outline a few that have been particularly important to the development of NOREX. But remember, the benefits of unconventional thinking will never appear unless you give it a try! In the long run, your organization will benefit with greater happiness and greater success for all!

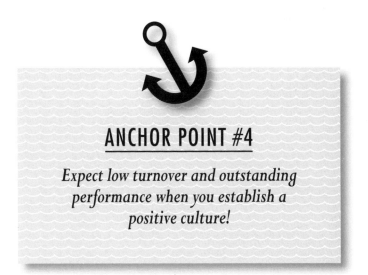

ANCHOR POINT #4

Expect low turnover and outstanding performance when you establish a positive culture!

WITH THE TIDE

Hire confident, smart, highly-experienced, and highly-skilled "hotshots."

AGAINST THE TIDE

Attract and hire nice people who fit into the culture, possess an energetic work ethic, a positive attitude, and the potential to perform at high levels.

CHAPTER 5

Attract Nice People

The *unconventional manager,* above all, recruits nice employees ... people who are pleasing and agreeable, polite and kind, and fit the culture.

Training employees to be nice is a very difficult (perhaps impossible) task. We have a saying at NOREX: "It is possible to teach a nice person skills, but impossible to teach a skilled person to be nice."

So we target prospective team members who are already nice and either have the skills or have the ability and enthusiasm to learn quickly.

It took us longer to build a team with this approach, but the result

> *It is possible to teach a nice person skills, but impossible to teach a skilled person to be nice.*

is a team that is enthusiastic and pleasant as well as competent. Here are some practical advantages of hiring nice people:

- **Positive Attitude:** You get a prevailing positive attitude in a group where everyone generally has a smiling face.
- **Attraction:** Nice people attract quality hires.
- **Harmony:** Nice people get along well with others and work together to achieve true synergy in developing new offerings as well as solving problems.

Ron —

"I am happy to know that retirement for you and Sandy is going great as you certainly deserve it – all of the CEOs of NOREX deserve it. I told Bob Klatt that when I think of great leaders I have met in 35 years of business I always think of Ron Haberkorn. Why? Because you had an eye for talent selection that few people have. From John Miller, Muench, Ditty, Shaleen, Bell, Beck (I could go on) the people you selected were all top-notch, you encouraged them to be successful and rewarded them when they were. Sincerely Ron, I know I told you this before, but you were an early influence on my leadership style."

Bob Koogler
Vice-President, Enterprise IT Infrastructure
Monsanto Company

NOTE FROM A CUSTOMER

- **Emergency Support:** Team members who experience a medical or family emergency receive a huge outpouring of support from co-workers who genuinely care about them.
- **Fun Place to Work:** Nice people are enjoyable to be around.

It is critical to go the extra mile in the recruiting process to ensure that you hire people who are compatible with the culture. To that end, we believe in being transparent about our unique culture in the recruitment process.

Wanted: Team players ... no **prima donnas** please! Accordingly, we give potential team members as many opportunities as possible to learn about our culture.

Wanted: Team players ... no prima donnas please!

OPEN HOUSE RECRUITING

At NOREX, the ideal format for recruiting has become the "open house." To generate attendance, we place ads in the local newspapers. However, unlike conventional help-wanted ads that emphasize the typical recruiting jargon, we stress high ethics and family values, and invite those interested to an evening open house at our office.

New hires are needed, but we recruit only the right people who value and support our culture. We don't want someone to join the company and suddenly say, "Whoa, this isn't what I wanted."

Our posture at these events is, naturally, unconventional. We are not trying to "hard-sell" people that do not believe in our ethics or culture. We are completely open and want to give them all the information we can about our organization. We strive to give prospects complete information so we can see whether they are truly excited about the opportunity to join us.

Two or three of our managers host these open houses and determine the level of the visitor's interest in our organization. We want potential hires to "kick the tires," see if they like what they see, and decide whether they want to continue the process.

From the attendees, we select candidates who are genuinely nice people and have the potential to be superior performers. We then invite them to our facility during working hours so they can meet as many of our team members as possible. We want them to spend time, ask questions, get a feel for the people they would be working with, and get a taste of every aspect of our environment. Only after the candidate decides NOREX is a good fit for them, do we make a formal offer to join the NOREX team.

OUR CULTURE VIDEO

To be sure our cultural message is consistent, we show the NOREX culture video during the open houses. It is essential that all prospective team members clearly understand our culture. In the video, we lay our cards on the table.

We're very cautious. Because we want to hire quality people: nice people, concerned people, service-oriented people. Candidates aren't being sold a lot of blue sky, nor do we gloss over the "real-world," hard work expected at NOREX. On the other hand, we do offer security, sanity, and a fun environment for all.

The trouble is, maintaining an unconventional culture is difficult to do on the fast track. Naturally, we could hire and staff more quickly if we lowered our hire-nice-people standard. Our objective is to perpetuate the enjoyable and highly-productive work environment.

In the process of building a team, it can be tempting to select an individual all-star with prima-donna tendencies. These applicants sometimes look too good to be true,

> *Quality people are our greatest assets!*

and in my experience they usually are. Highly skilled and capable, fine and good ... but they must be a team player and not expect any special privileges!

How do team members want to be treated? How do you want to be treated by those around you? You don't have to venture into the land of make believe to find the answers. You'll find them right in your own heart. In order to give team members the treatment you expect, you need to:

- **Respect them as people.**
- **"Ask" not "tell"** when you need help to

complete a project. They know who the leader is and don't need to be reminded. Be a manager who has humility.

- **Give them appreciation** for their effort and work. Let them know that they "make a difference."
- **Give them flexibility in their job** ... the belief that they can grow and learn new things to become even more productive.
- **Be open to their opinions.** You may not take them, but at least listen carefully and honor their desire to help.
- **Give them the knowledge** that they will not be punished for failures, but will be encouraged to learn from their mistakes.

Overall the needs of team members are relatively simple. In short, let these be your guiding principles:

- **Demonstrate a sincere** and heartfelt desire to create a squeaky-clean culture.
- **Treat fellow workers as equals,** or they never will perform as such.
- **Watch your language.** Rather than saying "my people," express the same thought referring to "our team." The words you use are critical to how people feel about you as well as themselves.
- **Don't get a reputation** for being aloof or

crabby. At every opportunity offer a sincere greeting with a friendly nod and a smile!

- **Recognize and respect** them as the principle movers and shapers of the organization, because they are! Could you do it alone?
- **Treat them like friends** and they will behave like friends.

MANAGING NICE PEOPLE

In terms of performance, NOREX team members are responsible for their own performance and their own hours. We try to do a real loose job of managing. We hire good people and ask them to be self-sufficient.

> *Treat them like friends, and they will behave like friends.*

Certainly, when new people first come on board, management is available to help train, accompany them on trips, and do whatever is necessary to help them get started. Over the long haul, however, we don't have management sitting around checking on people. We believe that "thin management" (not having too many managers around) really helps each of our team members have the freedom to perform.

ANCHOR POINT #5

A team of nice people results in cost savings, fewer management problems, and no prima-donna headaches.

WITH THE TIDE

Provide typical benefits and expect
everyone to be happy.

AGAINST THE TIDE

*"Knock the socks" off employee
expectations by providing numerous
above-and-beyond entitlements.*

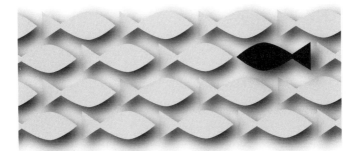

CHAPTER 6

Exceed Employee Expectations

Anything permanent is an entitlement. At NOREX, we offer the standard entitlements such as desk space, vacation days, health insurance, compensation package, etc. However, we deliberately try to "knock their socks off" by dramatically exceeding team member expectations with special NOREX entitlements. Many entitlements are very small, but every one sends a message of appreciation and respect to the team.

UNCONVENTIONAL ENTITLEMENTS

The following pages include a sampling of NOREX unconventional entitlements:

401K VESTING

Our 401K is *fully vested from the first day* of contributions. When a team member enters the plan, all NOREX contributions to the plan are 100% vested rather than using a partial vesting schedule based on years of service as most companies do. We've chosen this unconventional path because we do not want to put "hooks" in team members that encourage them to stay even if they are not happy. We try to create a great climate where they'll be happy for years to come. However, if a team member is not happy, we don't want them to stay with us just to get their 401K vested. The last thing any organization needs is an employee who says, "I would leave, except I need to wait for my vesting."

UNCONVENTIONAL FACILITY

We have gone *unconventional* with our facility in far too many ways to detail here (see Appendix 3 NOREX Building Features for full list). But here is just a small sample of our unconventional facility entitlements:

- Large 10-foot-wide spaces in the parking lot with double stripping to minimize door nicks on cars.
- Exercise room and equipment.
- Storage area for recreational equipment.
- Quality restrooms feature continuous circulation of hot water for quick warm water availability, showers, a maze rather than doors, and high-quality hand towels.
- Walls between offices are insulated for privacy.

- Courtesy umbrellas at front entrance ... take today, bring back tomorrow.

PRIVATE OFFICES FOR PRODUCTIVITY

Obviously private offices are not an option for all workplaces. From the beginning, NOREX has tried to maximize the number of private offices. In my early years I was with a large company where I shared an office with another individual. Every time we got off the phone and had a little success (or failure), we discussed it at length. Not very efficient!

There are two reasons to have private offices: One, to improve productivity since it helps us focus and get things done. And second, to exceed team expectations.

At NOREX the offices are not large, but all have a window to the outside. Team members appreciate the privacy and the fact that they can personalize their space.

Private offices improve productivity by helping us focus and get things done. And also exceed team expectations.

SHORTENED WORK HOURS

A few years ago we celebrated our success by reducing our team workdays to 7½ hours. We believe that a conscientious team will work hard and not cheat on each end of the day.

The shortened day has worked well. Occasionally we get a new person who thinks they can come in and goof off for the first half hour or knock off early at the end of the day. If that happens we explain to the team member the purpose of the 7½ hour day is to work hard and get a half hour off! We believe we are just as productive in a 7½ hour day as most organizations are with an 8 hour day.

THE MATTER OF BUDGETS

I have included budgets in this chapter because they can have a direct effect on a team. NOREX has budgets, but we treat them in an unconventional manner. For us they are simply guidelines. We don't turn down small expenses because they are not in the budget. Instead, if cash flow isn't what we had planned, we might put on a yellow light and slow expenditures, or put a freeze on non-critical expenditures. But, we generally don't use budgets as an *excuse* for not doing something. Sometimes we wish we had that excuse and could say, "Well, it's not in the budget," but philosophically, we don't operate that way. If it is beneficial to our customers or team, and affordable, we will do it whether it's a budgeted item or not. We always can offset, if needed, by holding off expenses in other areas.

> *We use budgets as a guideline ... not as an excuse for turning down a team member request.*

100% CLUB

Each year, NOREX holds a 100% Club incentive meeting

for our top sales performers and support team at a resort location. The three- to six-day meeting gives participants time for sales and personal-development training. It is also a good time for managers to have fun with the team. NOREX assumes all airfare and lodging expenses for participants and their spouses. Spouses are invited to attend all functions. Note: Because the IRS does not recognize spouses as a business expense, we pay team members a bonus to cover spouse expenses and taxes for the trip.

The 100% Club includes our administrative and support teams based on years of service. This has been a wonderful addition because they are key, key, key to our success! This is an unconventional move, as many organizations do not allow their support people to qualify for incentive trips. Including them has been really fun. We have a fabulous support team.

IN-OFFICE "ATRIUM" MEETINGS

Team member guests always are welcome at any office celebration, but we have a strict rule: absolutely no alcohol allowed in the building. At these meetings we recognize people who have made significant benchmarks. For example: years of service, sales achievements and project completion etc. Anything we want to celebrate! Occasionally we bring in sandwiches for lunch.

OFF-SITE TEAM PARTIES

We have an annual off-site Christmas Party for team members and spouses. Each attendee receives two drink tickets in order to minimize alcohol consumption. Also, we get to know the entire family, including kids and grandkids, at the NOREX annual summer picnic.

EXTENDED PERSONAL TIME

We have an extended personal time (EPT) policy that allows team members to take a percentage of unpaid time off on a sliding scale based on their years of service.

This policy was implemented when we had one individual that had been with us a long time and was getting close to retirement. We reasoned that he might be interested in taking a little more time off and deduct proportionally from his salary. He liked the idea.

Putting it another way, instead of getting a 3% pay increase for the next year, some team members take 3% time off instead. Though EPT was originally designed for people at later stages in their career, we have numerous younger team members who love it. It turns out to be a relatively small salary sacrifice, but a huge advantage to the team member.

EMPLOYEE OWNERSHIP

You'll notice that absent from the above list of entitlements is "team member ownership." There is a reason for that. When we started NOREX, I was fiercely independent … and still am. We could have taken on partners during our formative years when we were short on cash. Whether insiders or outsiders, additional financial resources would have been helpful. Instead I used a second, and later, a third mortgage on my personal residence and kept things simple.

I just didn't want to complicate my life. Many founders of conventional companies think employee ownership is crucial for employees to work hard and remain committed and "hooked" on working for the company.

But in many cases the stock ends up with little value and ends up disappointing participants.

The Unconventional Manager philosophy is the opposite. We don't want to hook people. We would rather pay employees well and recognize their contributions in other ways.

DON'T TAKE AWAY ENTITLEMENTS

At NOREX we adamantly avoid taking entitlements away from a team member or the team. Any team member would get upset or disappointed if we were to take away their private office or window. Deep down we all are just big kids. And if we get used to something we like, we are *profoundly* disappointed if it is taken away.

> *Do not trap yourself by unintentionally establishing new entitlements.*

So the lesson here is simple: Do not trap yourself by unintentionally establishing new entitlements. They will be very difficult, or impossible, to eliminate later without morale issues. Plan new entitlements by doing careful, long-range planning so they are never taken away.

IF YOU MUST

Should it become absolutely necessary to change or take an entitlement away, give it a great deal of thought. If possible do some long-range planning. Perhaps there is something you can do as a small offset when the actual change occurs. It is important to realize that the employee's disappointment of losing an entitlement is real and needs to be addressed. It could be as easy as going to lunch with them or a simple token gift and an apology.

> *Don't be such a tough manager that you show no respect for employees' feelings! Rather, show compassion.*

Don't be such a tough manager that you show no respect for employees' feelings! Rather, show compassion.

WHAT TEAM MEMBERS SAY

We receive many positive comments about the unusual culture at NOREX. Here are a couple of unsolicited notes from our team:

NOTE 1: *"NOREX is an incredible company to work for. Ron and Sandy have set the bar high for quality of life at the office. The atmosphere present at NOREX promotes healthy and happy attitudes, and it is the perfect compliment to the community. My family and I are very appreciative for the quality of life NOREX has provided us, and I look forward to a long career here at NOREX."* – ANONYMOUS

NOTE 2: "Many times I have stood before prospects and members alike and genuinely shared with them how proud I am of this company. How great it is to work for a company that I know will do the right thing time and time again. Company pride is a powerful and compelling sales tool.

You set a vision for an organizational culture that promotes a safe, healthy, above average environment, with honesty and integrity as the backbone and guiding principles for the company. This culture does provide a sound, successful, and rewarding career for employees, a solid value-added product, and service for its members, and a trusted and meaningful relationship for its vendors.

This is more than a mission or vision, it is the reality in our business every day in order for us to have a company that is authentic and sustainable. Our company treats all who interact with it (employees, members, vendors, communities, etc.) with respect and fair/equal treatment. The saying, 'Treat others as you would have them treat you' sums it up." – 12-YEAR EMPLOYEE

Try some of our unconventional principles and you will likely receive similar feedback from your organization.

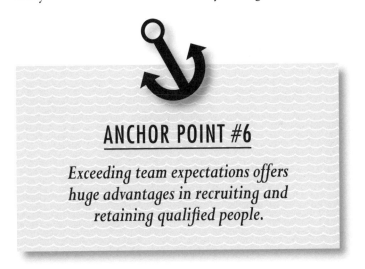

ANCHOR POINT #6

Exceeding team expectations offers huge advantages in recruiting and retaining qualified people.

WITH THE TIDE

Avoid special perks because it is too much trouble, and employees might come to feel entitled to them.

AGAINST THE TIDE

Open the soft drink machine for a "Never Again" perk and see what happens!

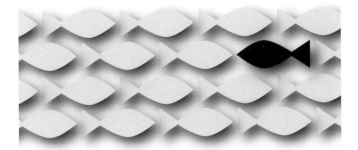

CHAPTER 7

Never Agains

The Never Again principle is, perhaps, the golden nugget of this book. It is likely more powerful than any of the other strategies of *The Unconventional Manager*. Never Agains provide instantaneous and lasting results, and they are fun for everyone. Surprise your employees with random perks at unexpected times. Give them a name such as "Never Agains" to clearly denote the one-time nature of the perk.

We stumbled on this incredibly effective yet simple idea some 15 years ago when Dan Alderson, now President of SSI Group, related this wonderful story to me:

He explained that he had a group of minimum-wage folks working in the back room. They were production workers who had done a particularly good job on a project. To show his gratitude, he went to the soft drink machine, unlocked it, and told the group to help themselves. It was a simple, inexpensive, one-time perk that simply delighted the group of workers!

His experience taught me an important lesson: Do something nice for an individual and he/she may or may not express appreciation. But do something nice for a group, and it will create a positive "buzz," plus give you and your management team a boost as well!

> *Do something nice for a group, and it will create a positive "buzz," plus give you and your management team a boost as well!*

We tried similar activities at NOREX for our employees, and they were a hit! They came to be known "tongue in cheek" as Never Agains, since we made it very clear these events were one-time events.

I believe this one idea has had a huge impact on the climate of our organization.

If you take nothing else from this book, please try this idea and remember: Never Again perks are not only fun for the team, but fun for management as well!

We have been careful to change the form and timing of these perks. We do them no more than once or twice a year, just to keep them fresh and fun. We also want to make sure they don't become entitlements!

There's a big difference between an entitlement and a Never Again perk. An entitlement is something the team has grown to expect as a permanent part of their employment. Never Again perks are random, spontaneous, and unpredictable; these perks cannot be relied upon as a regular occurrence.

There's a big difference between an entitlement and a Never Again perk. Never Again perks are <u>random, spontaneous, and unpredictable</u>.

The real point is that employees get the message that management cares about them and appreciates their many contributions.

SURPRISE, SURPRISE!

Remember, the purpose is to say "thank you" to employees for their outstanding work and show them that you care about them and the contributions they make to the success of the organization. The trick to the success of this program is to make it a surprise, make it fun, and make it different every time! Regardless of rank or length of employment, everybody participates.

Here are some Never Again perk ideas:

- A small bag of goodies on every desk with a thank-you note.
  LESS THAN $5 PER PERSON!

- Award everyone an hour or two of time off to be taken at their discretion.
  MINIMAL OUT OF POCKET COST!

- Take the group to a local mall and give them a

small bonus to spend on a two-hour shopping spree. Maybe require them to spend it on themselves. After returning to the workplace invite the group to your meeting room and have each "show and tell" what they purchased! A guaranteed good time for all!

$50 OR MORE PER PERSON!

- Have truckloads of pumpkins delivered to your building a week before Halloween and ask each employee to take home enough for their kids.

  LESS THAN $10 PER PERSON!

- Platoon the group and take them to play miniature golf. LESS THAN $10 PER PERSON!

- Have a carwash with the managers doing the washing. No out of pocket cost! Or give everyone coupons for a local car wash.

  LESS THAN $10 PER PERSON!

- Have an in-house movie day. Get a good movie and show it in the office conference room. Use multiple shifts in order to keep important job functions covered. Managers serve as ushers and hand out candy and popcorn.

  LESS THAN $10 PER PERSON!

> *Managers serve as ushers and hand out candy and popcorn.*

- Have a VIP welcome outside the

main entrance for everyone as they arrive in the morning. Set up a sound system and, with rousing music in the background, welcome each team member. All of the managers should form two single-file lines with space between for team members to walk through. As everyone arrives, the managers greet each person with a handshake, a pat on the back, and say "thank you for being a part of this fantastic team." Have a small bag of candy waiting with a thank-you note when they arrive at their desk. And consider getting the CEO or top manager of your organization to participate as well.

LESS THAN $10 PER PERSON!

• Ask each person to give you the name of a favorite charity and make a contribution in their name. A nice gesture for the team member, but if you are already giving to charity there is no additional cost!

THE CHALLENGE TO BE DIFFERENT

It is sometimes a challenge to dream up new and different activities, but I really believe, and I say this with all sincerity, we couldn't have a better team of people at NOREX! It is worth the effort to dream up new Never Agains, because the team is worth it!

Can We Afford It? Absolutely! Never Again perks can cost next to nothing and they make the workplace more fun for everyone. Your objective should be to convey a token thank-you. Any organization can afford a small bag of cashews or candy bar once in a while.

WHEN PERKS TURN INTO ENTITLEMENTS

A potential problem is that Never Agains, if done in a predictable pattern, can become expected. When they do, they lose their excitement, their luster, and their power to boost morale. They become an entitlement that must be given regardless of the organization's health and finances.

If a manager gives smoked hams to every employee as a Christmas gift for three years, and then in the fourth year the gift is changed to turkeys, likely there will be complaints. "What happened to the Christmas ham? I wanted the ham. Where's my ham?" It is human nature to develop expectations and to be a little disappointed when things change. If you are not careful a perk can evolve into an entitlement.

Please, please, try this strategy! Start with a small perk and see what happens. If you like it, continue! If you don't like it, don't do it again. My bet is you will be as enthusiastic as I am!

The Never Again concept is both easy and fun. Now simply do it! Open the soft drink machine, and see what happens …

ANCHOR POINT #7

*If you take nothing else from this book,
please try this idea and remember:
Never Again perks are fun
not only for the team, but are fun
for management as well!*

WITH THE TIDE

Employees perform only when pushed to their limits! It is okay to use reckless determination to "push the system" as necessary to achieve quarterly as well as annual targets. No excuses!

AGAINST THE TIDE

Managers need to understand that organizational results will vary from quarter to quarter and year to year ... get used to it!

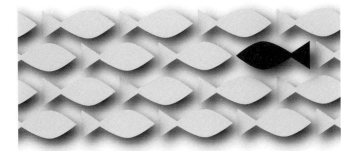

CHAPTER 8

Unconventional Goal Setting

Some readers of this book are likely working for very large organizations and wonder why any organization would subscribe to moderate growth objectives. Our small company may be insignificant in your eyes, but stay with me! In a simple way, our small company parallels my experience in a large organization.

WHAT IS YOUR MANAGEMENT PHILOSOPHY?

Two distinct philosophies are used in the workplace. Some call them "carrot" or "stick" (from the traditional alternatives of driving a donkey on by either holding out a carrot or whipping it with a stick) approaches.

Conventional managers tend to adopt the "stick" approach, believing that employees must be managed and pushed or pressured into performing. They use a "take no prisoner" path to success leaving destruction in their wake.

This behavior creates a climate for breaking organization rules and compromising ethical behavior.

> *This behavior creates a climate for breaking organization rules and compromising ethical behavior.*

Unconventional managers use the "carrot" approach, because they believe good people, with encouragement or incentives, have a sincere desire to perform at high levels. In fact, they believe that most employees enjoy achieving in a positive and enthusiastic low-pressure environment.

CONVENTIONAL GOAL SETTING

At the beginning of each fiscal year, senior managers of conventional organizations project revenue and expenses and, by extension, the bottom-line for the year. They get inputs from group and department managers for both revenue and expense forecasts.

Department managers make projections based on history and the *expectations of senior management*. If department managers choose to make moderate growth projections senior management may consider them "sand-baggers" or "slackers." In other words, department and group managers really do not have the freedom to forecast moderate growth if senior management expects aggressive growth. And, of course, senior management does agree to the final plan. So whose plan is it anyway?

Ultimately it is senior management's plan that has been "agreed to" by their department and group managers!

> *Ultimately it is senior management's plan that has been "agreed to" by their department and group managers!*

Generating revenue is much more difficult than incurring expenses. If the revenue forecast is too aggressive, the organization runs the risk of a mid-year panic to increase revenue and/or decrease expenses. Typically management doubles the pressure to generate more revenue and puts a hold on expenses. Excessive pressure is an incubator for ethical lapses. And if that doesn't work they have three choices: 1. Revise the revenue forecast and the projected results of the organization. 2. Use cash reserves to cover the revenue shortfall. 3. Cut expenses (limit travel, layoff employees, reduce compensation, etc.).

One of the large line items on the budget is labor and associated accounts. So if the revenue forecast was too aggressive the result is often budget cuts and layoffs.

> *Excessive pressure is an incubator for ethical lapses.*

If this cycle repeats

year after year, the revenue growth objectives have clearly been too aggressive!

UNCONVENTIONAL GOAL SETTING

At NOREX we intentionally establish moderate objectives, and we all enjoy achieving them.

> *"We spend too much time at the office not to have fun!"*

We work very hard. But we don't have a pressure-cooker environment. We don't have people afraid of being fired if they fail to make their quarterly goals. We have goals, to be sure, but NOREX is not, and never will be, a stick-motivated organization.

As we always say, "We spend too much time at the office not to have fun!"

Unconventional managers make every effort to hire and train the right people in order to achieve the organization's goals. Individual goals should be moderate so most employees can achieve them.

People don't *stop* working when they achieve their goals. And they don't *start* working only to achieve the goals. Instead, they are working because they are *committed and enthusiastic* about what they do. They enjoy exceeding objectives and going well beyond.

Once or twice a month, NOREX has a meeting to celebrate both individual and team achievements. Many of our team members have annual goals that are broken down by quarter. We celebrate these as well as many other achievements at these celebrations.

Any dummy can assign unrealistically high goals, but unless at least three-fourths of the team can achieve them,

> *Any dummy can assign unrealistically high goals, but unless at least three-fourths of the team can achieve them, they are too high.*

they are too high. Moderate, achievable goals are more fun for everyone!

In bad years management may have to "suck it up" and smile even though the objectives are not achieved. That's life!

MANAGEMENT RESPONSIBILITY

Remember that both Unconventional and Conventional Managers hold all the cards! Think about it. We decide who and how many get hired. We decide how much to spend on various priorities. And ultimately we decide on the goals for the organization and, by extension, the individuals.

So why is it that conventional management blames employees if goals are not met? Isn't management really to blame? Why didn't management hire more or better people? Why didn't management train and provide the necessary support to accomplish the priorities? Why didn't management set achievable goals? Or why weren't industry projections considered when setting the plan?

Managers need to understand that organization results

will vary from quarter-to-quarter and year-to-year. Get used to it!

Why should the team be subject to budget cuts and layoffs when management misses their forecast? Shouldn't management be the first to take earnings reductions and layoffs when results fall short? Absolutely!

REAL LIFE EXAMPLE

During a recent year, NOREX revenue was good but short of historical growth trends. In addition, expenses were very high because of decisions management made earlier in the year. The options were to lay off employees, borrow dollars on organization assets, reduce ownership income, or all three. I chose to both significantly reduce ownership income as well as borrow on assets. This was my "penalty" for being too aggressive planning for growth.

THE BOTTOM LINE

If managers adopted this approach and took full responsibility, over-aggressive forecasting would stop! After all, it is easy to make aggressive forecasts. I have done it many times only to realize that not meeting the forecast was not the fault of our team! After all, we hired the best, and we trained and supported them. If it was their fault, then by extension, it was my fault!

Unconventional organizations go against the tide and commit to moderate growth each year and stick with it. Moderate objectives eliminate the mid-year panic and the resulting roller coaster for the team. In good years the objectives will be substantially exceeded! In fair years the objectives will be achieved!

Let's change the paradigm in this country: When management forecasts are not achieved, it is management's fault! Do not blame the team for the failures of management!

> *New paradigm: When management forecasts are not achieved, it is management's fault! Do not blame the team for the failures of management!*

Management and ownership must flex (financially and otherwise) to achieve maximum employment stability.

EMPLOYEE GOAL SETTING

Even if a team member has an outstanding year, the goal for next year should not be a "stretch," but rather in line with others on the team. To do otherwise penalizes the outstanding performer.

With modest objectives, NOREX team members enjoy achieving 150%, 200%, and more! They just do not stop at 100%.

Because they enjoy exceeding expectations they will continue to strive for higher performance levels even after they achieve their initial goals. Moderate objectives will allow them to be excited about achieving 125% or 150% of goal!

This philosophy swims against the tide because conventional managers believe they must "pressure" the team to achieve high performance levels. Unconventional managers believe that people respond best when they achieve on their own terms, not because they are driven by pressure objectives.

GROUP GOAL SETTING

Management must be careful not to aggressively increase group goals over a previous outstanding year. For example, if productivity increased 10% last year, then maybe a 5-7% increase over last year's goal may be appropriate.

> *With modest objectives, NOREX team members enjoy achieving 150%, 200%, and more! They just do not stop at 100%.*

Forcing exceedingly aggressive growth rates the following year will put the group on a treadmill and penalize them for their outstanding performance the prior year.

In our small organization, it has been very easy to understand. Rather than pressuring our managers to take on aggressive revenue objectives, we often cut the revenue projection to make our overall plan realistic and achievable. We still move into each year with plans to maximize growth! It does not take "pressure" objectives to encourage the team to achieve, but rather they enjoy exceeding objectives and going well beyond!

ANCHOR POINT #8

When corporate and individual goals are reasonable, they will be exceeded, and the work atmosphere will brim with success and enthusiasm!

WITH THE TIDE

*When times are tough,
cut out the peanuts.*

AGAINST THE TIDE

*Instead of cutting the peanuts,
add cashews!*

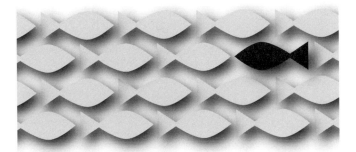

CHAPTER 9

Exceed Customer Expectations

It seems like such an exceedingly simple concept:
Treat your customers *more than* fairly and with respect, integrity,
fairness, and compassion, and they will respond with loyalty.
Plus, you'll create friends and have satisfied customers for the
life of your organization. Yet how many times have you person-
ally dealt with organizations that were much more interested
in their own welfare than yours?

At NOREX, we believe total satisfaction for all customers is the reason we exist. That's why we go the extra mile
on their behalf.

Customer expectations are easy to exceed. Find out where
their parade (needs) is going ... then get out in front and
pretend you are leading it!

> *Customer expectations are easy to exceed. Find out where their parade (needs) is going ... then get out in front and pretend you are leading it!*

CONVENTIONAL COMPANY CUSTOMER SERVICE

Many conventional organizations express allegiance to customer needs but still offer only "lip service" to first-class customer service. Take telephone communications, for example. Second only to face-to-face customer meetings, the telephone at one time was the primary communication tool between company and customers.

Today, however, most of us find ourselves in a voicemail jungle. Telephones are answered by machines offering a menu of choices based on your reason for calling. Rarely do you to speak to a real human being. After much switching and transferring of the phone call you find the destination of your call is outsourced to foreign countries thousands of miles away. This is all done in the interest of cutting expenses, certainly not to provide superb customer service!

New millennium Internet enterprises simply exacerbate the problem. On the Worldwide Web, real answers seldom seem available as companies are intent on hiding behind email addresses and providing customers with one-size-fits-all FAQs instead of making it easy for customers to reach a real person. Again, this is done to save money ... certainly not to provide superb customer service!

These organizations believe if they cut all the expenses possible, they will be more successful. However, deep cutting without considering the impact on customers and employees is foolish.

AIRLINES IN THE CUT, CUT, CUT MODE

One of the airlines I frequently use has done everything possible to cut expenses, and as a result, antagonized their crew members and customers as well. It is not hard for me to imagine a budget cutter somewhere saying, "Cut out the food, cut out the peanuts, charge for the food, and we will save millions of dollars each month!" And a big pat on the back goes to the budget cutter! Are you kidding me? I seriously question any decision to reduce customer service!

Airlines have huge fuel, labor, equipment, and facilities expenses. My guess is that one of those expenses could "hiccup" far more than the minor savings on customer ser-

> *Outstanding customer service pays for itself!*

vice items. Plus, outstanding customer service pays for itself! Even though the benefits are "soft," managers must understand that the organization is abundantly rewarded in employee and customer loyalty.

On the other hand, when customer services are cut, every passenger on every plane is impacted. Every crew member on every flight is impacted with passengers who are not in the happiest mood. And at the same time passengers are complaining over back fences throughout the country about how cheap the airline is! Are these airline employees proud of their company? I doubt it.

> *Had the airlines increased customer service during tough times, might more customers be loyal to them today?*

The last thing any organization should do is cut customer service. Had they increased customer service during these times, might more customers be loyal to them today? They could have added cashews instead of cutting out the peanuts! Might their company-wide employees have had pride in their company and enjoyed what they were doing a bit more? How can they ignore the value of these soft, but important benefits to their customers AND employees?

PEOPLE ARE THE FOUNDATION!

The foundation for NOREX first-class customer service is our team of quality people who are dedicated to serving. Here are some examples of how NOREX exceeds customer expectations:

- Our receptionist is a real person speaking clear English who makes every effort to locate the specific person requested by the caller. The customer has the option to call directly to the individual's extension if they want.

- Our unconditional guarantee of customer satisfaction is real.
- Customers receive unhurried, personal attention from a friendly team member who is truly receptive to helping them. Complaints or special needs are an OPPORTUNITY rather than a chore. The customer is always right!
- Our customers become our friends because our team truly cares for their needs.

> *Our customers become our friends because our team truly cares for their needs.*

GIVING ADDITIONAL VALUE

Over the years we have continually added new dimensions to our service, always without additional charge. Many companies seek to increase revenue and profitability by offering add-ons for additional fees. We swim against the tide. NOREX has no add-on "for fee" services. For example, we have added a number of services since our founding, and none have been charged for:

- National Conferences with spouses program – no vendors
- Regional Conferences – no vendors
- Telephone Conferences – no vendors

- An on-line repository of research papers and data received from our customers

The "no vendors" aspect is emphasized because some companies include vendors and have them sponsor events. We swim against the tide by not including vendors. Our customers appreciate the no-vendor policy because:

- Frank and honest discussions would not take place if vendor "observers" were in attendance.
- Customers do not want to be added to a vendor mailing or prospect list.
- Customer focus is on information exchange with other IT professionals. Not spending time with vendors.

HOW TO EXCEED CUSTOMER EXPECTATIONS?

Many "unconventional organizations" (including NOREX) go above and beyond to provide unexpected and exceedingly outstanding customer service. Excellent customer service on a daily basis is essential.

The real test comes when something from your organization goes wrong that negatively affects or could affect the customer. This provides an organization a perfect opportunity to make a real impact! In the blink of an eye, the entire record of past service with the customer is at risk depending on how the current problem is handled. It will make a long-lasting impression on your customer. It is up to you what the impression will be. Here are a couple examples of making a positive out of a negative customer-service situation:

During a NOREX incentive trip at the Fairmont Orchid Resort on the Big Island of Hawaii we experienced a false fire alarm at 3:00 a.m. The entire wing of the hotel lumbered down the emergency staircase (many from the 5th floor) to the outside. The weather was good, but after waiting about 30 minutes for clearance, we all trudged back up to our respective floors. A huge inconvenience when you are on a dream vacation! We were a little tired in the morning, but we still experienced a wonderful day in paradise. We arrived back to our room in the afternoon and found a note with a plate of Hawaiian goodies from Ian Pullan, the general manager, apologizing for the false alarm. Although we would have preferred no false alarm, the apology and goodies from Ian certainly left us with a "sweet taste" (pun intended) regarding the hotel. This was absolutely exceptional and beyond-expectations customer service!

> *Absolutely exceptional and beyond-expectations customer service!*

Even the U.S. Post Office is trying to achieve superb customer service. Recently I received a letter in the mail that had been damaged by a postal machine. The Post Office could merely have taped it up and delivered it. Instead they inserted it into a plastic bag with large print saying, "We Care" at the top and a printed note of apology! Even the Post Office cares! What a nice gesture.

Here are important elements present in the previous examples:

- They were truthful and open about what happened!
- They took full responsibility! No weasel wording that it somehow was someone else's fault!

- They were unabashedly apologetic!
- They were timely with the action taken!
- In the case of the hotel a token peace offering was given!

Emergency or not, never, never "fib" to anyone, much less a customer! Be totally open with them and share exactly what went wrong, whether it is your fault or not. Customers understand that some-

> *Emergency or not, never, never "fib" to anyone, much less a customer!*

times "things happen," and if you react properly they will forgive you. No customer or problem is big enough for you to present a cover up! Lying is not only patently wrong, but your team will lose respect for you as well. **Don't even think about it!**

NOREX EXCEEDS CUSTOMER EXPECTATIONS

At NOREX we receive many unsolicited notes from our customers thanking us for the help we have given them. We have removed both person and company names to respect privacy. Our team takes great pride when we receive these notes. Here is what NOREX customers say about exceeding their expectations:

NOTE 1: *"I feel that the tone of the interactions I've had with NOREX (both through the introductory e-mails and the teleforum itself) have been welcoming, professional, non-intimidating and collabora-*

tive. I appreciate that. After this, my first teleforum, I'm enthusiastically spreading the word about NOREX within our IS division!"
— NORTH DAKOTA CUSTOMER

NOTE 2: *"Thank you sooooo much ... I just want you to know how pleased I am with NOREX as a whole based on the information you make available. It is fastly becoming my FIRST go-to resource. I feel your staff is very caring and responsive. It's great that everyone takes ownership in making sure information is understood and complete. You all are great!!"* – TULSA CUSTOMER

NOTE 3: *"Thanks (name removed for privacy), you are one of the most responsive people I have ever worked with — please pass this comment on to your manager! The information you supplied previously was most helpful, but we will take anything else you receive based on the questionnaire you sent out."* – ATLANTA CUSTOMER

NOTE 4: *"I wanted to let you know how pleased I am to work with you. I have worked in my job for 6 years and have used NOREX to not only purchase, but sell equipment also. I recently sold some equipment that was not too marketable. However, you were able to find a buyer in a short time. You are always quick to respond to my requests and a follow-up is done to see how the transaction has gone. You have saved me hours of work time. This is important to my company and me."* – WISCONSIN CUSTOMER

NOTE 5: *"I have been thinking about what will be different when I retire. One of the first things that comes to mind is NOREX. You are an organization like no other. You are special. Everyone is so friendly and you try to make everyone feel welcome and a part of everything which goes on at the conferences. The friendships I have gained over the last 9-10 years will never be forgotten. I will certainly miss coming to the conferences. I thank you all for the organization that you are. Don't change a thing. I wish you all happiness and good health. God Bless."* – MINNESOTA CUSTOMER

> **Always give first-class service. Happy customers are quick to compliment employees, fostering great morale.**

NOTE 6: *"In my 44 years with John Hancock and now 9 years retired, I have both, then & now, never been associated with a company and people that have the values set forth from the top of the house down. These values are so evident that they spread over to the people that NOREX has contact with. That is why I have always said Sue and I are very proud to be part of the NOREX Family."* – BOSTON CUSTOMER

NOTE 7: *"NOREX is a valuable resource by bringing diverse companies together to share the expertise and knowledge of their IT professionals. The NOREX document repository helps eliminate having to reinvent the wheel. The biggest draw is the regional Forums and the weekly TeleForums which enable the membership to discuss issues which are important to them. I am glad NOREX exists."* – MISSOURI CUSTOMER

Here is a story written by a NOREX team member about a customer in New Orleans after the 2005 Katrina Disaster:

"Hurricane Katrina damaged many of their facilities. They stayed in contact with NOREX through their ordeal. Their senior IT executive provided a TeleForum presentation to the NOREX membership in December 2005 sharing their recovery process. Nearly 100 members participated on the call and many, many more are still reading the transcript and learning this "real world" IT experience.

Due to their devastating loss, NOREX offered all members impacted by Katrina that we would either return their membership dues or give them a no-charge extended membership! Not one member asked us to return any renewal payment. However, they did accept

the gift of an additional renewal year due to the budget loss they experienced." – NOREX TEAM MEMBER

BUILDING A MUTUAL BOND

In today's highly competitive world ... filled with well-educated employees and savvy consumers ... the secret to achieving lasting success is a conscientious effort to avoid the model of a highly-leveraged organization with huge roller-coaster rides for the employees, customers, vendors, and management. Plus, we

> *Honesty is the single, most important factor in the success of an organization.*

live in an age where openness and honesty are apparently unique. It pays to be up front at all times. Honesty is the single, most important factor in the success of an organization.

THE UNCONVENTIONAL STRATEGY FOR KEEPING IN SYNC

By listening carefully, you can keep your organization in tune with customer needs and expectations. And, surprisingly, customer expectations are fun and easy to exceed.

- **Maintain a responsive and honest** customer environment.
- **Provide a 100% customer satisfaction guarantee** of your service and products.
- **Provide immediate enthusiastic feedback** for every customer request ... no matter how large the challenge.

- **Commit and lead** your organization's energy and enthusiasm to provide exceptional service to your customers.

When you treat customers with fairness, respect, integrity and compassion, you will, in this day and age, exceed their expectations!

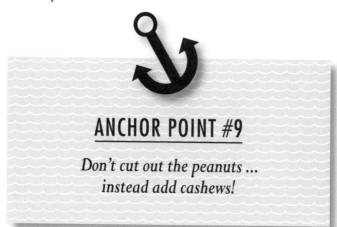

ANCHOR POINT #9

*Don't cut out the peanuts ...
instead add cashews!*

WITH THE TIDE

Aggressive growth is required to
"target" the window of opportunity!

AGAINST THE TIDE

*There is no window.
In this wonderful country
opportunity is unlimited!*

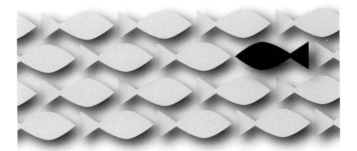

CHAPTER 10

Baby Steps & Giant Strides

Remember the tortoise and the hare, the fable attributed to the Greek storyteller, Aesop? The story, you'll recall, concerns a hare who one day ridiculed a slow-moving tortoise. In response, the tortoise challenged his swifter adversary to a race. The hare soon left the tortoise swirling in a cloud of dust. He was so confident of winning the race that he decided to take a nap halfway through the course. When he awoke, however, he sadly discovered that his competitor, crawling slowly but steadily, had already won the race.

While there are a number of morals that can be drawn from this fable, one is obvious to us: Slow and steady wins the day. It is neither necessary nor prudent to go as fast as you can, regardless of the nature of your undertaking.

We see this principle at work everywhere in our lives: Too much + too fast = disaster. If marathon runners begin the race at too fast a pace, they will create an "oxygen deficit" that cannot be repaid, and they will likely fade to an uncompetitively slow pace at the crucial finish. The strategy of successful investing and saving is built entirely on the principle of slow, but steady growth. And in organizations, no principle could be more relevant: steady, sustained improvement wins every time.

THE PERILS OF AGGRESSIVE GROWTH

All sorts of problems crop up when you try to grow too fast. There may be a tendency to hire "the best you can find" rather than holding out for the right "fit." Cash may be in short supply, causing pressures to compromise the culture. Growing too fast often causes dollars to be squandered in search for the quick buck. The organization may begin to struggle to train new people and meet delivery dates. Customer complaints boil over, and you don't have time or staff to satisfy them properly. The quality of products or services begins to suffer. And of course you're working such unconscionably long hours that your body and your spirit sags.

THE NOREX UNCONVENTIONAL EXAMPLE

NOREX is not a get-rich-quick operation. Our goal never was to take the business "fast track" in order to maximize value, make a quick exit by selling the company, and pocket a ton of money. We are in it for the long haul, paying our bills along the way and vigilantly protecting the future of our team.

Using slow and steady as our mantra, modest growth is acceptable. Our approach of setting attainable and sustainable growth goals for both individual team members as well as the organization has helped NOREX avoid the "roller coaster rides" experienced by many companies.

"GROWTH" BY A NOREX TEAM MEMBER

"One thing that I've heard you say many times is that "modest growth is acceptable." I believe your approach of setting "attainable and sustainable" sales and growth goals for both individual employees and the company has helped NOREX avoid the pitfalls experienced by many companies. I think one shining example how your "modest growth approach" has served NOREX well was during the dot-com era.

During the 90s many companies in the technology industry were trying to win a race up a mountain in order to claim a trophy at the top. In contrast, NOREX wasn't concerned about getting to the top of the mountain or claiming the trophy. NOREX wanted to enjoy the hike and set out at a steady pace with an eye on the trail ahead.

Modest growth provides a stable working environment when others have been forced to lay off staff or close their doors.

In their haste many companies took unnecessary chances. They also had trouble taking their eyes off the trophy at the top of the mountain. While running up the mountain and gazing at the trophy, companies failed to notice a loose rock on the trail and fell off a cliff before reaching the top. NOREX on the other hand saw the loose rock, sidestepped it, and kept marching up the mountain.

NOREX has experienced modest growth in most years, and

perhaps more importantly, has been able to avoid falling off a cliff. NOREX has been able to provide its employees with a stable working environment when other companies have been forced to lay off staff or close their doors." – NOREX TEAM MEMBER

DOT-COMS BECOME DOT-BOMBS

Of course, we all know what happened when the market and the business world discovered that most of the dot-coms would never show a profit. Stock prices tumbled precipitously. Billions of dollars were lost in the stock market. Many organizations went bankrupt. Tens of thousands of employees were laid off. It has taken years to recover from this turbulent era.

NOREX lived through this horrendous cycle. We weren't concerned about getting to the top of the mountain or spearheading growth at any price. We call NOREX a "baby-step company." We learned our baby-step approach the hard way in the early days by getting a little too ambitious with some new initiatives. The result was that we were forced to lay off some team members. A very painful time! This experience cemented our belief that modest growth is acceptable and that jackrabbit growth is very risky. We continue to choose stability over rapid growth.

LOCAL TORTOISE AND HARE EXAMPLES

Some companies that started in our community about the same time that we did are now out of business because they were leveraged too highly and were unable to survive the tough times.

Managing is like driving on ice! Minimize quick turns and braking. Instead, be consistent and make small, careful adjustments for maximum group morale!

> *Managing is like driving on ice ... be consistent and make small, careful adjustments.*

Here are actual illustrations of hare-type companies that started in our community:

EXCELSIOR-HENDERSON MOTORCYCLES

A shining example of overreaching one's financial grasp is the legacy of Excelsior-Henderson, the motorcycle manufacturer that enjoyed a brief renaissance right in our Minnesota backyard.

The original company produced motorcycles from 1912 until 1931 from a plant in Detroit, Mich. The company was merged in 1917 with Schwinn, the bicycle maker, which also made Excelsior brand motorbikes. Schwinn abandoned the motorcycle business in 1931 and Excelsior-Henderson ceased to exist.

Excelsior-Henderson Motorcycle Co. was begun anew by two brothers who in 1994 secured the rights to the defunct but quality trademark. Using investor dollars and subsidies from local government, they built a gleaming, state-of-the-art factory that many believed overextended their upstart business. Their original (and some say over-ambitious) business plan scheduled motorcycle production to begin in December 1998 with projected annual sales of 20,000 units.

But that snazzy new building didn't begin to manufacture new motorcycles until the spring of 1999, and they sold fewer than 2000 over the following summer and fall. Ouch! It proved to be too much investment too soon.

Lackluster sales resulted in Excelsior-Henderson laying off a large portion of its workforce. At the close of 1999, the company filed for bankruptcy. What appeared to be a wonderful business plan failed, probably because of too much too fast!

> *Other organizations got publicity and recognition for their aggressive plans while we were just small and chugging along.*

THE BANK START-UP THAT FELL DOWN

Or take the case of the bank start-up in our community that went bust, taking the money and the faith of some of my close friends and relatives who invested. This new venture built a new building and took on a presence that rivaled the 90-year-old bank already in town. By trying to make it on the fast track, they failed. Two years later the bank was sold, and the bank president went to jail!

While we could cite example after stunning example, I think you get the picture. Fast-track growth feeds one's greed and ego, but is often unnecessary and very risky to employees and investors. Also, the pressure makes the organization susceptible to breeches of honesty and integrity! Slow and steady wins the day and increases the probability of success.

AND THE TORTOISE FLOURISHES . . .

In the early days it was sometimes disheartening for us to see other organizations getting publicity and recognition for their aggressive plans while we were just small and chugging along. We continued to swim against the tide and not only survived, but thrived while those high-growth, highly-leveraged companies failed with a big splash!

OWN OR RENT?

Not only has NOREX taken an unconventional position on growth, we also have moved slowly and surely at improving our headquarters.

We have heard many times that businesses should lease space and invest all funds in promotion and development of the organization. This seems to be the prevalent philosophy in the

We scraped together a small down payment, took out a Small Business Administration loan, and went to our local banker for help.

business community with managers saying, "We don't want to be in the real estate business."

Again we swam against the tide and took a totally opposite approach! After a few years of leasing space, we scraped together a small down payment, took out a Small Business Administration loan, and went to our local banker for help. From then on we have been making building payments while accumulating equity at the same time!

We believe the benefits of building ownership have been huge:

- The team feels a real sense of permanence and pride in our building.
- We have been able to tailor the building to the needs of our team in every respect.
- Building maintenance is never an issue. We do a first-rate job of caring for the building.
- We have no landlord to raise our rent or approve building changes we may want to make.
- We have maximum flexibility to expand the facility consistent with our needs. No need to pay for expansion options which may be available either too early or too late based on our actual needs. We expanded our first building two times and then built an entirely new facility.
- Our new property is large enough to enable us to double the size of our facility.
- The original building was paid off years ago, and this asset gave us the financial muscle that enabled our bank to give us more attractive terms for financing the new building.

The bottom line is to take growth slowly and steadily. Bite off no more than you can sensibly chew. And don't worry if your plant and equipment are not top of the line at the beginning. If you grow slowly and steadily, you'll be able to afford what your operation needs.

THE UNCONVENTIONAL APPROACH TO EQUIPMENT

Many organizations lease everything, including equipment and leasehold improvements. They believe they are leveraging their financial situation better by leasing rather than buying.

Again NOREX does just the opposite. We pay cash for everything! We purchase all of our com-

> *"There is no payment lower than zero!"*

puters and office equipment. We have a saying: "There is no payment lower than zero!" And when something is paid for, it's paid for! If there is a downturn in business, there are no payments vying for scarce dollars. We own everything.

BUYING COMPUTERS AND OTHER EQUIPMENT

For many years the NOREX management team took internal criticism for not putting computers on every desk more quickly. We could have taken either the conventional manager or the unconventional manager approach.

The conventional manager might hire an outside consultant to write a computer technology plan and implement it. The problem we had with that approach was that we are adamant that anything we implement is committed to and understood by our team. We didn't want to "stuff it down their throats." Rushing things along often causes a "push back" from those responsible for implementation.

By contrast, we took the unconventional tack and took it slow and steady, baby-step style. If our first step works, we move on to the next, gradually implementing the system that fits our needs with the complete cooperation of the team.

By using this process, we have created a computer network with better hardware and software than would have been available had we jumped in feet-first and implemented the entire system ten years ago. And ultimately we have saved significant expenses using the baby-step approach.

ANCHOR POINT #10

Slow and steady "baby steps" provide a stable environment for the team AND customers.

WITH THE TIDE

The organization should have
overwhelming priority in
employee's lives.

AGAINST THE TIDE

*A stable family-friendly
environment is a critical element of
organizational success.*

CHAPTER 11

Family Preservation

NOREX swims against the tide because in many respects we treat our team exactly the opposite of the way many (maybe even most) organizations do. Many ignore family and focus only on the employee. We don't.

We created a culture that fosters family cohesiveness. We discourage overtime or weekend "presence" when team members should be at home with their families. Off-site events include spouses.

This chapter outlines some specific family-preserving elements of the NOREX culture.

> *We discourage overtime or weekend "presence" when team members should be at home with their families.*

> *When spouses know other team members and their families, it creates a climate that minimizes the potential for office romances and helps to protect the family.*

INCENTIVE TRIPS

NOREX has a 100% Club (incentive trip) each year to celebrate the contributions of the team members ... spouses are always invited. An employer from my past did not allow us to invite spouses to an event like this. In addition, the sales office I worked in had a rule that no spouse was allowed in the city during the incentive trip. Why might this be? Might the parties be too wild to allow spouses to be there?

When spouses know other employees and their families, it creates a climate that minimizes the potential for office romances and helps to protect the family.

In the history of our organization, we have had no office affairs (at least none that we know of). We hope and pray that no NOREX family will suffer a marriage problem or divorce because of any NOREX activity.

CHRISTMAS CELEBRATIONS

NOREX has an annual Christmas Dinner for team members and spouses at a local restaurant or country club. Two drink tickets are given to each attendee. NOREX has a "light/ modest" drinking policy. Over-drinking by either a team member or a spouse is not acceptable at NOREX functions.

OFFICE PARTY PROTOCOL

At NOREX, no alcohol is allowed in our facility ... ever! Occasionally we will have a sub-sandwich lunch with soft drinks in the office to celebrate a major team accomplishment. But again, no alcohol. Spouses are welcome to attend these internal celebrations.

FAMILY SUPPORT WHILE TRAVELING

If a team member is traveling, we suggest they call home every night. We consider this a business expense. It is difficult to be out of town alone making sales visits. Some days there are appointment cancellations, bad weather, and frustrations following a map in a strange city. It is not a glamour job, so they need family support!

The support team members get from their spouses and family is HUGE!

We consider the family, the spouse, or significant other to be our sales person's "sales manager." The family typically pumps up the team member when they have had a difficult day. It is really the spouse that gives them moral support. They are the real sales managers. The support team members get from their spouses and family is HUGE! And ... the call supports the family as well!

FAMILIES ARE FIRST

We offer flexibility when the family has a need, and the team member must be there. The first reaction of our managers is, "Go take care of your family." Here is a note received from one of our team members after a NOREX off-site social event:

> "I am not sure you and Sandy recognize all the little things you do to make NOREX such a great place to work. I would like to share an example that may seem small to you, but was very meaningful to us. When Michele and I had to leave the Christmas party last Saturday night because Olivia got sick, you and Sandy, John and Steph, and the entire Executive Team encouraged us to get home and make sure Olivia was doing okay. Then the NOREX team at our table packed up our meals and sent them home with Brad Miller (who happens to be our neighbor) and he delivered them to us."
>
> In some companies a newly promoted employee might need to think twice before approaching the CEO to inform him about needing to leave a company function to take care of a family issue. You and Sandy do such a wonderful job of letting the NOREX team know where our priorities should be "faith and family first" that you make it easy for us to make good decisions when it comes to balancing family and work.
>
> Thank you for creating such a caring culture at NOREX! Merry Christmas." – NOREX TEAM MEMBER

EXTENDED PERSONAL TIME

Our extended personal time policy (chapter 6) is very much a part of our commitment to family preservation. I mention it here again just to emphasize its importance to families!

INCOME STABILITY AND TIME WITH THE FAMILY

Conventional organizations seek aggressive growth objectives, and then hire the people to meet the objectives. The result is a pressure-filled organization requiring team members to give up family time. It is easy to be overly aggressive and assign "stretch objectives" for the organization! When the objectives are not met, employees are

> *Modest growth projections offer far better employment stability for families.*

often laid off with an obvious impact on their families.

The key is assigning goals that are reasonable and achievable. Swim against the tide … modest growth projections offer far better employment stability for families.

VERBAL ABUSE & SEXUAL HARASSMENT

Our commitment to the team is, "If you are offended in any way, report it to your manager. No sexual or verbal harassment of any kind will be tolerated from anyone … including *customers.*"

Hiring nice people (chapter 5) goes a long way toward avoiding sexual harassment in the workplace. They seem to be particularly attuned to their own behavior and how it affects those they work with. They treat others as they wish to be treated.

The legal issues are important enough, but even more crucial is the impact such behavior can have on team members. Time wasted in harassment complaints, or worse yet, lawsuits, firings, and replacement of offenders, is time that cannot be spent on advancing the primary function of managing a successful, growing organization.

NOREX is not a locker room environment. We have a no-profanity workplace. Some businesses might allow a superstar to get away with bad language. But no one is superstar enough to compromise the culture at NOREX.

CUSTOMER BEHAVIOR

We don't want NOREX team members to be subjected to sexual harassment, verbal abuse, either by fellow team members or by our customers. We make it very clear to our team that if any customer says anything inappropriate to them that they don't have to take it. They can tell the customer exactly how they feel about the comment, and NOREX will stand behind them when contacting the offending customer.

> *It doesn't matter how big the customer is; we are not going to let the customer compromise our team members in any way.*

And that means *all customers*. It doesn't matter how big the customer is, we are not going to let the customer compromise our team members in any way.

Team members also can be put in awkward situations on the road. It doesn't happen very often, but it is always a concern to me when we have a group of people travel to conference sites around the country. At our very first conference in 1980, one of our team members was a single young lady who was, perhaps, a little naïve. A group of nice customers (primarily men) invited her out to dinner. I made it very clear to her that she had no obligation to go with them. It was not necessary for her to spend any extra time with them at all. In fact I really discouraged it, and still discourage such activities.

OFFICE ROMANCES

Our advice to married team members: DON'T EVEN THINK ABOUT IT.

If two single team members want to date, we don't encourage it, but we do not unilaterally disallow it either. Still it doesn't take a rocket scientist to know that when office romances between singles go sour, the workplace will invariably suffer, and that should be avoided.

If one or both of the employees is married, however, the case is cut and dried. The team member would be asked to discontinue the behavior. If they want to remove themselves from the situation, we would help them leave the company (with a severance package) if they want. The reason is simple. These issues are disruptive, and we want to do all we can to protect families.

I believe our recruiting practices help nip these problems in the bud. The thorough process we go through in recruiting people gives employees a clear view of our culture and expectations. Sure, potential candidates who have walked away might have said, "NOREX is a little too limiting for me." That is fine with us. That is the purpose of our process. Our goal is to hire people who are in line with our culture and expectations.

WHY FAMILY FRIENDLY WORKS

Affairs, alcohol, and harassment are huge distractions in any workplace. By providing a positive, family-friendly, and safe environment, NOREX team members are free to work without distractions. Spouses know we are looking out for their families' best interests and become cheerleaders for the entire organization. The result: Our team members are upbeat, focused, and productive!

ANCHOR POINT #11

Provide a positive, family-friendly, safe environment. The team will be upbeat, focused, and productive!

WITH THE TIDE

Make sure no one takes
advantage of the organization.
The best defense is a good offense.

AGAINST THE TIDE

Don't get hung up on principle.
Seldom is there a molehill
worth the negative energy
and cost to pursue!

CHAPTER 12

Don't Make Mountains Out Of The Wrong Molehills

Since the start-up of NOREX in 1980, we have never been involved in a lawsuit! We conscientiously try to treat all of our customers, vendors, and team members more than fairly in every situation.

Yes, there have been times when our management team suppressed feelings of frustration or anger. Instead we were flexible and resolved

> *A decision to take NO action is sometimes more critical than a decision TO act.*

issues while they were small. We intentionally have chosen not to elevate any issues to a lawsuit level, even when we believed we were right. And boy, has this saved us tons of time, negative energy, and money. Our saying is, "Don't make mountains out of the wrong molehills." If you choose to make mountains out of every molehill, you could be in lawsuits half the time!

A decision to take NO action is sometimes more critical than a decision TO act.

CHOOSE NOT TO GO THERE

Sometimes it frustrates our team members that we aren't tougher when somebody "does us wrong." But in the long term, this posture allows us to put energy toward helping our customers. We avoid expending negative energy trying to "get even" or pursuing a litigious course which seldom results in any clear-cut winner.

The easiest time to resolve a lawsuit is before it takes place.

During one of my previous employments, we had a lawsuit that lasted for years and put a pall over the entire organization. Digging up documentation, giving depositions, and court appearances are not fun activities and are very time consuming. At NOREX, we simply choose not to go there.

Most settlements become a compromise when finally resolved, and both sides lose (legal fees, judgments, and time spent). And even more importantly, lawsuits would be a huge distraction from our business mission.

It's easy to come up with reasons why a particular molehill is different and must be acted upon. But the easiest time to resolve a lawsuit is before it takes place. The unconventional way is to satisfy the complainer and don't get involved in a lawsuit.

SLEEP WELL

And another advantage to *The Unconventional Manager* philosophy is that NOREX has an excellent image in the community. We can meet anyone anywhere on positive, agreeable terms. We have no enemies, so we can sleep at night!

> *Don't get hung up on principle. Seldom is a molehill worth the time and negative energy to pursue.*

NOREX avoids legal issues by being fair, or more than fair, with everyone we touch: team members, customers, vendors, and the community. If someone complains, we actually listen to what they're saying. If they've got a concern, we want to solve that concern before it gets to any level that would even come close to a legal issue.

Don't get hung up on principle. Seldom is a molehill worth the time and negative energy to pursue.

ANCHOR POINT #12

*Avoid getting so aggressively
postured that you can't back off.
No lawsuits, no hassles!*

WITH THE TIDE

Concern for the community
or other causes are at the
bottom of the priority list.

AGAINST THE TIDE

Being a good neighbor is an
important part of what ultimately
defines an organization.

CHAPTER 13

Vendors, Community & Country

It is no surprise that many conventional organizations shirk their responsibilities to everyone but themselves. What the *unconventional manager* realizes is that being a *good* neighbor is an important part of what ultimately defines an organization.

TREATING VENDORS AS FRIENDS

Conventional managers often care little about the vendors that provide them with the goods and services that help them succeed. In fact, many treat vendors as a "necessary evil" and abuse them by showing little or no respect.

At NOREX, we practice the time-honored Golden Rule

... "Do unto others as you would have them do unto you." That might sound like overworked hyperbole, but we mean every word of it with respect to all of our relationships ... including relationships with our vendors.

Our vendors are very important to us. We believe that the more fairly they are treated, the more *committed* they are to helping us over the long term. Accordingly, we don't incessantly scour the marketplace to see if we can shave a nickel or dime from the price of our vendors' products. The truth is, at any given time you can probably beat the price of any vendor. The trouble is, there's no guarantee that two months later, the new vendor won't raise prices as high, or higher, than the original vendor.

> *We pay vendor bills when they are received ... well before they are due.*

We pay vendor bills before they are due. We do not "vendor hop" but instead value the long-term relationship of vendor loyalty and service.

If a vendor is fair and doing a quality job with excellent service, we are very, very loyal. The result is they are loyal to us by giving us the best price and best service possible. Plus, a huge amount of time is saved by not having to evaluate and re-evaluate vendors! Of course, if a vendor ever betrays our trust, the NOREX relationship will promptly be terminated.

Incidentally, NOREX is a vendor to our customers and we appreciate their loyalty to us! As they say, "what goes around comes around."

VENDOR BILL PAYMENT

An important facet of maintaining superior vendor loyalty is paying invoices on time, every time. Many organizations are known for slow payment of accounts payable in order to "operate on the float." This approach is in direct conflict with the Golden Rule and for that matter, most anyone's definition of fair play.

It is fun to swim against the tide by paying our bills every week, whether they are due or not. We get appreciative feedback from our vendors for being "quick pay." Plus it gives our team pride in our organization knowing that we pay bills upon receipt rather than playing games with cash flow. We get positive feedback from the community as well.

CHARITY FOR ALL

The notion of giving is so fundamental to good citizenship that its benefits hardly need to be argued. In a nutshell, whatever the gifts are,

> *NOREX has no management-sponsored charities that cause team members to feel obligated to donate.*

large or small, they pay huge dividends to the recipient as well as the organization.

NOREX has no management-sponsored charities that cause team members to feel obligated to donate. Giving is very personal and individuals should give when, to whom, and how much they want ... without pressure or coercion from the workplace.

Past organizations have taught me that certain national charities invade the workplace. When that happens, employees feel obligated to give so the organization can achieve certain goals. The result is that employees feel coerced by the organization to give. Employees resent this approach.

At NOREX we set up a charity budget based on a generous dollar amount per team member per year. We significantly exceed that amount during outstanding financial years.

We definitely believe that team member charitable giving is important. We just don't think they should have to contend with charitable pressure in the workplace. We don't allow any fund raising on the premises because it's impossible to separate being encouraged to give vs. being shamed into giving. No soliciting of team members is allowed.

One exception: Children of our team members put out sign-up sheets for Girl Scout® cookies, local school fundraisers etc. We just could not turn down the kids!

COUNTRY AND COMMUNITY

Providing fun and well-paying jobs and supporting vendors benefits our community and country.

> *Providing fun and well-paying jobs and supporting vendors benefits our community and country.*

After the 9/11 terrorist attack, many individuals, and businesses "pulled in their horns." The uncertainty of the times, together with the forecast of a general business down turn, caused many organizations to enter a holding pattern.

But *The Unconventional Manager* did just the opposite. It was important to both the local and national economies to continue with business as usual. At NOREX we continued to purchase equipment, hire more people, maintain our previous level of air travel, and launched a local "Buy Now, Fly Now" campaign complete with pins and window stickers.

> *It was fun swimming against the tide and a privilege to help our community, state, and federal economies!*

In addition, we also broke ground on a new building in the months following 9/11! In partnership with our city government and our bank, NOREX acquired land and built a 16,000 sq. ft. building with room for an additional 16,000 sq. ft. building on the same parcel. We knew the future of the U.S. was strong and growing, just as we knew *our* future was bright. It was fun swimming against the tide and helping, in our small way, both the community and country.

The city, bank, and NOREX partnership was likely made possible because of our payment record, reputation, community involvement, and good citizenship during the years prior. The result was merely a natural outcome demonstrating the benefits of "doing the right thing." And everybody benefits!

The construction of our new facility produced direct and indirect jobs, including laborers, manufacturers, and other suppliers to the project. Though small in the scheme of things, the state and the nation saw increased revenue due to these jobs and other economic activity that this project produced.

It was fun swimming against the tide of conventional wisdom and a privilege to help our community, state, and federal economies!

NO TAX GAMES

We don't ask our team members to play games in order to help NOREX avoid taxes. Naturally, we take every tax deduction that we are entitled to, but we don't ask our accountants to scour the tax laws in search of spurious loopholes for questionable deductions. One of the companies I worked for in my younger years played tax games at year-end in order to report certain results to the stockholders, etc. How can an employer do this and still expect squeaky-clean integrity from its employees?

Employees do not want to be put in the position of playing "tax games." As a by-product they lose respect for their organization.

> *Employees do not want to be put in the position of playing "tax games." As a by-product they lose respect for their organization.*

Our approach makes NOREX something that the team can be proud of. We are good patrons of our vendors. Plus we are good citizens of our community, state, and country!

In addition, it is fun for our team members to hear positive community feedback on the quality organization that we are.

ANCHOR POINT #13

Be a good neighbor.
You succeed when your vendors,
community, and country succeed.

WITH THE TIDE

One must be tough to be successful!
Fairness, respect, integrity and
compassion just will not work in all
situations.

AGAINST THE TIDE

*Uncompromising fairness, respect,
integrity and compassion <u>in all
situations</u> will lead to a long-term
successful life and career.*

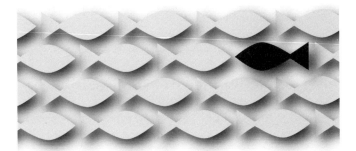

CHAPTER 14

The End Is Your Beginning

It is easy to formulate a body of principles that, if dutifully followed, will improve your organization and by extension, your life. It is easy, perhaps, to convince you of the wisdom of *The Unconventional Manager.* What is hard, however, is to get you to turn this wisdom into action and actually put it to work in your own organization.

My hope is that this book has encouraged you to think about conventional vs. unconventional practices, and compare them to what is actually going on in your organization. Experience how "swimming against the tide" can lead to some fun ways of improving employee morale and productivity in your organization. Will things then be perfect? No way! But things will definitely be much better than what conventional organizations experience!

Do you remember the anchor points? For your convenience, here is a recap of those principles:

THE PRINCIPLES OF "THE UNCONVENTIONAL MANAGER"

OVERALL PRINCIPLE: **The road to enduring success is paved with fairness, respect, integrity and compassion!**

⚓ ANCHOR POINT #1: The unconventional manager principles outlined in this book will reduce the probability of scandals in your organization.

⚓ ANCHOR POINT #2: Focus first on people and then profit/productivity. Long-term sustainability will result.

⚓ ANCHOR POINT #3: Relax and sleep at night with a clear conscience knowing that you are absolutely committed to doing what is right in all situations.

⚓ ANCHOR POINT #4: Expect low turnover and outstanding performance when you establish a positive culture.

⚓ ANCHOR POINT #5: A team of nice people results in cost savings, fewer management problems, and no prima-donna headaches.

⚓ ANCHOR POINT #6: Exceeding team expectations offers huge advantages in recruiting and retaining qualified people.

⚓ ANCHOR POINT #7: If you take nothing else from this book please try this idea and remember: Never Again perks are fun not only for the team, but are fun for management as well!

⚓ ANCHOR POINT #8: When corporate and individual goals are reasonable they will be exceeded, and the work atmosphere will brim with success and enthusiasm!

⚓ ANCHOR POINT #9: Don't cut out the peanuts … instead add cashews!

⚓ ANCHOR POINT #10: Slow and steady "baby steps" provide a stable environment for the team AND customers.

⚓ ANCHOR POINT #11: Provide a positive, family-friendly, safe environment. The team will be upbeat, focused, and productive!

⚓ ANCHOR POINT #12: Avoid getting so aggressively postured that you can't back off. No lawsuits, no hassles!

⚓ ANCHOR POINT #13: Be a good neighbor. You succeed when your vendors, community, and country succeed.

⚓ ANCHOR POINT #14: Remember, the path to enduring success is via integrity, fairness, respect and compassion.

THE MAJOR MESSAGE

The overriding theme of the anchor points and this book is simple. The world is comprised of interdependent agents: employees, customers, vendors, and community. When these various independent units work together ... each respecting the others' rights and obligations ... everybody wins!

Vendors sell goods and services at competitive prices. Customers get a fair and honest deal. Employees experience a stable and enjoyable career. Shareholders and lenders get honest value for their investment. And the community prospers!

The rising tide of goodwill raises the boats to benefit all.

> *The rising tide of goodwill raises the boats to benefit all.*

This book identified some unconventional principles that can help you achieve the goals outlined by this win-win paradigm. I am just an average guy who had the courage to go against what I thought was the conventional approach to management. And if I can do it, so can you!

YOU CAN DO IT

No matter what your background, no matter your mission, your life does not have to be controlled by tradition and the multitude of conventional practices those traditions thrust upon you. Being unconventional with fairness, respect, integrity and compassion is the best and most fun way to live. And at the same time it makes you feel a little macho or courageous to "swim against the tide"!

If one should achieve great fortune, but compromises fairness, respect, integrity and compassion, it is not true success! Mother would not be proud!

If you've already started to make changes, terrific! Keep it going. It takes courage to swim against the tide. And if you're still standing on the sidelines, get started ... now, today ... and stick with it! It takes daring.

> *If one should achieve great fortune, but compromises fairness, respect, integrity and compassion, it is not true success!*

It takes guts. It takes wisdom. The choice is yours. Now ... dive in, get your feet wet, and enjoy *swimming against the tide!*

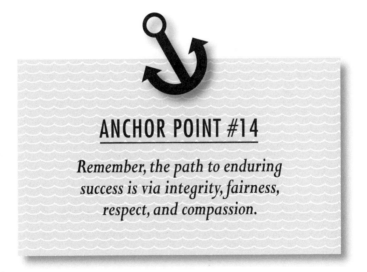

ANCHOR POINT #14

Remember, the path to enduring success is via integrity, fairness, respect, and compassion.

APPENDIX 1: THE NOREX PLEDGE

To Members/Customers: Total member/customer satisfaction is the reason we exist, and we go the "extra mile" on their behalf. All of our energy and enthusiasm is focused on exceeding expectations.

To Vendors: Vendor appreciation and fairness is critical to a predictable future for our vendors and NOREX. We pay vendor bills before they are due. We do not "vendor hop." Instead, we value long-term relationships of loyalty and service.

To Team Members: A stable family-friendly environment is a critical element of our present and future success. Employment fairness and stability outrank profit as our primary goal. Adequate profit (not maximum) will result. Financial performance will vary from quarter to quarter and year to year. It is the obligation of management/ownership to "flex" as required to achieve maximum employment security.

To Country and Community: We are deeply thankful to our country and community for fostering an environment where NOREX can thrive. We show our appreciation through positive involvement in the community and annual charitable giving of over 5% of profits before tax.

APPENDIX 2: TEAM BELIEF IN NOREX PLEDGE

This is an anonymous team survey we took to see what kind of "buy in" we had on the NOREX Pledge. There are a number of areas we need to work on.

MEMBERS/CUSTOMERS

1. A major portion of our energy and enthusiasm is focused on exceeding our member's expectations. **83% Agree**

2. Total satisfaction of those we serve is the reason we exist and we go the "extra mile" on their behalf. **95% Agree**

VENDORS

3. We treat vendors with appreciation and fairness to help create a predictable future for our vendors and their employees. **100% Agree**

4. We pay vendor bills before they are due. **100% Agree**

5. We do not "vendor shop" but rather choose to reward loyalty and service from vendors with long term relationships. **92% Agree**

TEAM MEMBERS

6. A stable family friendly environment is a critical element of our present and future success. **95% Agree**

7. Employment fairness and stability outrank financial objectives as our primary goal.
90% Agree

8. Team members are asked to be highly ethical and will therefore, be praised (not chastised) for bringing to light areas where our organization may improve ethically. **84% Agree**

COUNTRY AND COMMUNITY

9. We are deeply thankful to our country and community for the opportunity of making a living by helping those we serve and we show our appreciation through positive involvement in the community. **100% Agree**

10. We are committed to generous annual charitable giving. **100% Agree**

MANAGEMENT AND OWNERS

11. Our management and owners protect the ethical and moral environment in the best interest of those we serve and employ. **90% Agree**

12. Conservative decisions will be made with maximum team input to ensure a stable employment setting.
68% Agree

13. Financial performance will vary from quarter to quarter and year to year and the management and owners "flex" their incomes as required to achieve maximum employment security. **70% Agree**

GENERAL

14. I would recommend NOREX to others for career opportunities. **100% Agree**
15. NOREX is an excellent place to work. **100% Agree**

ANONYMOUS TEAM MEMBER NOTES ATTACHED TO THE QUESTIONNAIRES:

- *I am proud to be part of an organization with such a pledge.*
- *I'm proud of the document and of the way we live up to it.*
- *An excellent place to work!!!*
- *I feel blessed to work at NOREX.*
- *NOREX is the "best ever"!*

APPENDIX 3: NOREX
BUILDING FEATURES

The following list includes some of the "Exceed Team Member Expectations" features of the NOREX building:

PRIVATE OFFICES: The building has private windowed offices for all team members. Each office has a view of court-yards, woods, pond, grassy, or landscaped areas.

PARKING LOT: The parking lot has large (10 feet wide) spaces with double stripping to minimize door nicks on cars. Excellent lighting provides maximum safety at night. A lighted flagpole displays the American Flag 24 hours each day. There is a small storage garage for team members' bicycles and other recreational equipment.

RESTROOMS: Continuous circulation of hot water provides quick, warm water availability in the restrooms. Automatic controls on lavatories and toilets provide both convenience and sanitary conditions. Entrance to restrooms is via a maze (no doors) which provides convenient, safe (no doors to run into) and sanitary entrance/exit. The women's room has a small private lounge area. There are showers, lockers, and benches in both restrooms to facilitate exercise programs. The toilet stalls have floor-to-ceiling walls for maximum privacy. Heavy-duty individual "Country Club" style paper towels are used to minimize tearing and messy restrooms.

HEATING/AIR CONDITIONING: The building has 16 zones for maximum comfort control. Thermostats provide automatic switch over between heating and air-conditioning at any time of the year, depending on the needs of the individual zones. For example, a hot day in the spring will automatically trigger air conditioning in any zone that needs it. Three zone categories are available to accommodate team member's temperature preferences for normal, warmer than normal, and cooler than normal. Team members select their preference and the zone thermostats are set to accommodate these differences. A special automatic fresh-air-intake system provides maximum air quality and the health benefits of clean air.

PHYSICAL FITNESS: Across the street is a public sidewalk with a 2-block walk to a park where there are walking/biking paths etc. to facilitate exercise programs. The exercise room has major physical fitness machines (treadmills, weights, etc.), a wall of mirrors, a rack-mounted TV set for viewing and a pleasant view of the south courtyard.

LUNCH ROOM: Has two refrigerators with ice makers, one soft drink machine, two microwaves, filtered water and a view of the south courtyard.

GENERAL FEATURES: All offices have outside windows. Parking areas are in front of the building in order to preserve the best views for team member offices. Upgraded fluorescent lighting throughout the building is designed to minimize shadows and glare. Upgraded ceiling tile provides 20% better acoustics than the standard ceiling tile. Nine-foot ceilings provide an open and roomy feeling in the offices. Walls between offices are insulated to preserve quiet spaces. Every office has a window to a hallway so other team members can make a judgment on whether to interrupt an activity or not.

FUN AND SIMPLE FEATURE: Umbrella rack at the front entrance with courtesty umbrellas ... take today, bring back tomorrow.